TAKE A WALK ON THE WILD SIDE

MILIA'S BIG DAY

BY **THEA FELDMAN**

© 2006 Discovery Communications, Inc.
Animal Planet and logo are trademarks
of Discovery Communications, Inc.,
used under license. All rights reserved.
www.animalplanet.com

Design by E. Friedman
Contributing consultant Dr. Robert W. Shumaker
of the Great Ape Trust of Iowa

© 2006 by Meredith Corporation.
First Edition. Printed in the USA, bound in Mexico.
All rights reserved.
ISBN: 0-696-23290-1
Meredith® Books
Des Moines, Iowa

Milia was so excited! Today she was finally grown up enough to take a turn watching over the herd during their afternoon break. She could hardly wait until they would stop and rest. Milia was ready!

Fast Facts

Plains zebras live together in a group (7 to 10) called a herd. Each herd has one adult male, called a stallion. The herd includes several adult females (mares) and their children (foals).

As the herd set off to look for a good grazing spot, Milia walked behind her mother, Damali. Damali always led the way across the African savanna that they called home.

Fast Facts
The oldest mare generally takes the lead when the herd looks for food and water. Her foals follow right behind her, followed by the next oldest mare and her foals. The stallion is last.

A strange stallion approached the herd soon after they stopped in a nice grassy place. The stranger wanted to take over the herd. Milia's father, Erasto trotted over and tried to get the stranger to leave. He wouldn't budge, so Erasto had no choice. He had to protect his herd!

Fast Facts

A zebra can communicate with body language. Some examples include the position of their ears, whether their mouths are open or their teeth are exposed.

Milia watched her father fight the stranger. Finally, the stallion turned and ran away. Erasto chased him just to make sure he kept going.

Fast Facts
A kick from a zebra's hind legs can do serious damage. A zebra will kick another zebra in a fight and in defense against a lion or other predator.

Things quickly settled down and the herd began to munch and crunch the green grass. Milia stood beside her mother. She felt safe as she rested her chin on Damali's back. Milia knew that one day soon she would be old enough to leave the herd, but today she was right where she belonged.

Fast Facts

When a female plains zebra is about 18 to 24 months old, she leaves her first herd. She joins another stallion's herd and may remain there for life.

In the heat of the afternoon, the herd needed to get some rest. Finally, it was Milia's turn to stand guard! She was very excited. While the herd slept, Milia looked for predators. As she watched the grass-covered savanna, Milia turned her ears toward every noise—even the slightest noises—to make sure she did not miss anything.

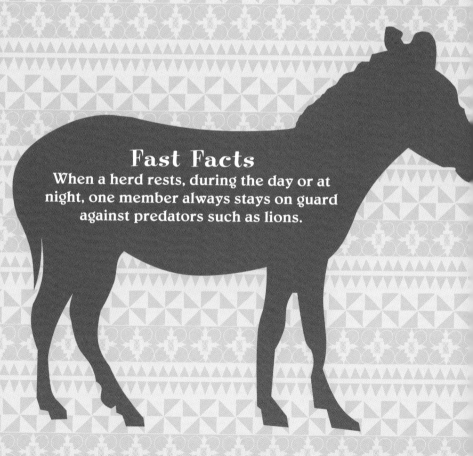

Fast Facts
When a herd rests, during the day or at night, one member always stays on guard against predators such as lions.

The savanna was quiet and a cool breeze blew through the tall grass. But . . . wait! What was that? Milia wasn't sure, but she thought she heard something. Was it a hungry lion? Milia didn't wait to find out! She quickly woke the herd and in a flash of hooves, off they went!

Fast Facts
Zebras can run up to 35 miles an hour. They are members of the horse family and have strong legs and hooves.

The herd ran and ran. It was very frightening for Milia. She had never given the danger signal before. Had she done it correctly? Was everyone all right? When they all felt safe, the herd stopped and looked around. Where was baby Ato? He was missing!

Fast Facts
A newborn foal can stand within 15 minutes of birth. By the time it is one hour old, it can run and keep up with its herd!

Erasto went to look for young Ato. Milia was afraid. What if something happened to baby Ato? She would feel terrible. Suddenly Milia saw Erasto's head over the tall grass, but she could not see Ato. As Erasto came closer, Milia saw Ato bound into the open! Ato was safe! He had become separated from the herd and had hidden in the tall grass when a lion passed by. Everyone was very proud of Milia and Ato.

Fast Facts

Every zebra has a different pattern of stripe
A foal learns to identify each member of
its herd by its stripes, smell, and voice.

Now that Ato was back safely with the herd, Damali stood beside Milia to let her know everything was all right. They quietly grazed and nuzzled one another.

Fast Facts
Plains zebras spend about half of their day eating. They prefer to eat grass, but they will also eat shoots and leaves. They may travel up to 12 miles a day searching for food.

When everyone had enough to eat, Damali turned and led the herd to a watering hole. It was time to drink some cool, refreshing water.

Fast Facts

Plains zebras usually drink water from a watering hole at least once a day. Because zebras require water, they are never far from it.

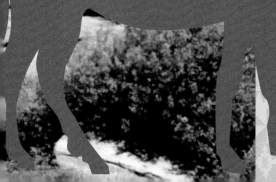

As Milia swallowed a mouthful of water she looked up and thought about the day. She had done it. She watched over the herd and kept everyone safe. She was a grown-up zebra now! It had been a big day!